# Demon Straightening
## Poems
## Pauline Plummer

First published December 1999 by IRON Press
5 Marden Terrace
Cullercoats
North Shields
Northumberland
NE30 4PD
Tel/Fax: (0191) 253 1901
E-mail: seaboy@freenetname.co.uk

ISBN 0 906228 73 5

Printed by Peterson Printers, South Shields

© Pauline Plummer 1999
Typeset in Comic Sans 12pt

Cover design by Peter Mortimer
Book design by Kitty Fitzgerald

IRON Press books are distributed by
Signature Books Representation Limited
Sun House, 2 Little Peter Street, Manchester M15 4PS
Tel: (0161) 834 8767
Fax: (0161) 834 8656
E-mail: admin@signature-books.co.uk

*Front Cover Photograph shows a Buddhist destroyer of death united with his female, Wisdom, (Tibet, 18th Century).*
*Back Cover: Box, by Chris Madans.*

Photo: Catherine More

**Pauline Plummer**, former fruit picker, chauffeur, human rights worker, community worker, typist, cook, filing clerk, pub cleaner, mother, was born in Liverpool (an Irish /Welsh mixture) but has lived in Middlesbrough since 1983. Her first collection *Romeo's Café* was published in 1993; *Palaver*, a collection of poems with paintings by Annette Chevallier followed in 1998. Her poems have been published widely and she has read on Radio 4, Tyne Tees TV, Sierra Leone TV. She currently teaches on the MA Creative Writing at the University of Northumbria, is Poet Laureate in Middlesbrough and an editor with Mud Fog Press.

## Acknowledgements

These poems have appeared in *Stand, Rialto, The Independent, Pennine Platform, Scratch, Blade, Smoke, Seam, Smith's Knoll, Mslexia, Envoi, Red Herring, Orbis, Tees Valley Writer, English Today* and on the web site of the Dublin Writers and have appeared in exhibitions at The Hatton Gallery, Newcastle, Middlesbrough Gallery of Art, Plymouth Arts Centre and Salford Art Gallery, in *Palaver* (Scratch Press), and in the anthologies *A Hole Like That* (Scratch Press), and *The Blue Room Anthology* (Diamond Twig Press).

I would like to thank the University of Northumbria for its support (particularly Joan Day); also Nessa O'Mahoney and Andy Croft for helpful comments on the work.

## *Running Order*

| | |
|---|---|
| 7 | Looking like a Barmaid |
| 8 | Curve |
| 9 | Travelling North from Middlesbrough |
| 11 | Whatever you say say nothing |
| 12 | Street Life |
| 13 | Postcard Home |
| 15 | North Sea, November 1991 |
| 16 | Brighton Rock |
| 18 | Picking Conkers in the Cemetery |
| 19 | Commadaties |
| 20 | Asylum ---shelter, refuge, sanctuary |
| 21 | Edgy |
| 22 | Demon de Midi |
| 24 | Brian Keenan's Orange |
| 25 | Writing in Prison |
| 26 | Stalked |
| 28 | FengShui |
| 29 | John Clarkson |
| 31 | Death in the Province of Freedom |
| 33 | The Life of a Sailor |
| 34 | Straw into Gold |
| 36 | Sweet Bleeding Heart |
| 38 | Learning to Talk |
| 39 | Getting my Tongue Round Escaveche |
| 41 | Too many Cowboy Films |
| 42 | Uncles and Aunties |
| 43 | Some small Thoughts about Swimming |
| 44 | Archeology in Ireland |

## Running Order (cont.)

| | |
|---|---|
| 46 | Looking for Myth |
| 47 | A Cool Hand |
| 48 | Babe |
| 49 | A Stanza for Peter |
| 50 | In the Salon |
| 51 | Breathless |
| 52 | Sailing on Single Beds |
| 53 | Mother and Daughters |
| 54 | Mike at Fifty |
| 55 | Lonely Hearts |
| 56 | Slicing Aubergines |
| 57 | Swimming in the Irish Sea |
| 58 | Walking Out |
| 59 | R & R |
| 60 | Dunfermline |
| 61 | Café Tinto |
| 62 | Porque Tenemos Deseo? Because we are alone |
| 63 | Buying a Blouse that Fits |
| 64 | You are the one my Womb Loves Best |
| 65 | What Like is Love ? |
| 66 | Swansong for the Womb |
| 67 | Strictly Tempo |
| 69 | News from Burkina Faso |

## Looking like a Barmaid

Looking like a Barmaid
has been a disadvantage
as a poet; *I didn't think
you'd be, you'd be, so large!*

I don't waft in to read, pale,
porcelain, intense
My large freckled hand
usually grips a Guinness.

## Curve

Midnight and the soft click of letters
as they slide onto a screen; the light
is a paper moon and I'm pressing metre
onto morpheme, crisp like the starred sky.

What keeps me earthbound, sisal ropes
ragged but tough, their wiry bodies
asleep, pirating dream sloops
sails ablaze to shoot the tide before me.

The screen glows with the words torn
from memory or scrutiny, harsh, bright,
to be risked, scraped, cut and daubed
till what has to be said is said right.

The screen curves me beating a word
into a song, a prayer, a freed bird.

## Travelling North from Middlesbrough

At seven am
in my rear-view mirror
a cobalt sky
a cloud of sandalwood behind a sinuous line of hills.

I pass
the night shift young
falling from the Rat Ride of thin dresses and sharp trousers
into their stargazing bedrooms.

The bakery girls
roll up their floury arms, freckles like sultanas.
The Queen of Diamonds shakes up the sleeping school
with her mop. A tinker's horse
Crops the priest's garden.

Over Newport Bridge
riding its spine of blue steel
a heron unmoors and veers across the slurry
towards the oil rigs.

Past the prison's
fluorescent bulging walls, its pale sloping skylights,
its breeze block cloisters.

Beyond the dingy fields
the sea is an anklet of diamonds cut to forty facets.

Behind the husk of fire and phials of smoke
the light of houses squeezed into a saw's serrated edge,
phosphorescent with flocks of spotlights,
the steel pipes,
hissing steam,
a line of snake.

*Whatever you say say nothing*


The train tore through England; West
to North East. We watched the price
of houses falling through the sleet.
Under the tables we re-arranged our feet.

The chorus of shurrups sit downs,
you're stupid ,turned me round
to see the  mother, Bristol sounds
softening the abuse, her switched off
face. Her man was crossbow tense,
young, lippy, with a grebe's quiff.
He hit the plump legs of baby Grace.

Then clenched his fist into a weapon
a serpent's head and held
it up against her nose - her eyes were old
with what would happen.

I couldn't keep the words from out
*Don't punch the baby* - and the carriage froze
as he in fury leaned across the seat
and invited me to taste his fist.

*I'm her father* - the waves from his words
jammed the frequencies in the heads
of people turning up their walkmans.
His shame would later burn as punishment.

Pauline Plummer

## Street Life

The girls trot in shiny high heels
curtain nets draped over heads
for a wedding in the alley.

Little mothers they fling round kid
sisters whose screams wreck
the sleep of old men and blackbirds.

A boy worships our dog, his neck
pressed into mongrel fur,
kneels, arm resting along the back.

A dog loves you whatever you are
suffers the same pain
when kicked by giant's anger.

A neat old boy pulls back a curtain
sees himself playing tig and catch
till tea time when his mother calls him in,

He knows that all things pass;
his single life, his childlessness.

## Postcard Home

From inside this green womb
With its Christian clouds and indigo skies
Smelling of damp grass and wild herbs
Where every footstep crushes something living,
Where an expressionist heron wings it, dead cool
Over the beasts of the field
Grinding mouthfuls of mallow and buttercup
And the earth slowbakes into a breadcake
And dappled deer nap among cabbages -

I want to tell you about
Cranes stabbing the sky
Of our talismans of steel bridges
Of dead docks where ships rust,
Like the men decomposing in the bookies.
About giant phials, pipes and cooling towers
With the subtle curves of Japanese ceramics
Of the eternal bonfires of flares and burning gases
Of molten steel effervescing into a lake of brimstone.

Of a paradigm of two up two down polished houses
In grids of streets and alleys,
Of Edwardian drinking palaces,
Of Victorian turrets and porticoes .

Of a serpentine, arsenic river
Of its treeless and muddy trajectory
Past futuristic follies of half finished oil rigs
Ablaze with spotlights.

Pauline Plummer

To tell you also
About estates imploding
Of the women too young to have such lived in faces
Rifling the jumble for some half decent clothes for the kids

Of the young spilling out of the night clubs
Happy with flirting and dancing
How the electricity of their excitement
Can short circuit into a smashed bottle in the face

Of how easy it is
To strike up a conversation at a bus stop
Of neighbours who bring libations of tea,
Or great bales of greens from allotments
Or how on a Saturday afternoon
Worshippers press into the stadium
For the symphony of football
To levitate the town.

(Written before the opening of the new Cellnet Football Stadium)

## North Sea, November 1991

Moon

      Mercury

           Menopausal

The O of a mouth
Forceps marks on the soft skull.

      An opal eye.
      A clock melting in the mist off the North Sea.

A liquid moon lapping
with the eyelid flicker of winter seas -
framed through the soft focus lens
of a windscreen greased by drizzle and fog
sliced by the soft metronome of wipers
droplets sizzling into diamonds in the oncoming headlights.

Moon

      anchored and floating
in a bay strung with factory lights
ladders of houses up to the motorway
torn through the dene where the small claws
of frozen leaves curl in the molten light
of a month clotted with soaked dreams.

Pauline Plummer

## Brighton Rock

*Human nature doesn't change. Like a stick of Brighton Rock you bite all the way down and still read "Brighton".*
- Graham Greene

In the moneyed streets,
gay antique dealers
sip gin, dreaming of owl bites,
tears melting the mascara,
salt on the cheek,
salt on the spray on the pier,
where escapees from London,
day-trippers floating in deck chair dresses,
lips red as fruit machine strawberries,
tuck yesterday down their bras
and lark about pissed on warm beer
in pubs with pianos twanging like suspenders,
screaming feelies in the tunnel of love.

Brighton,
also starring the locals in bit parts,
pickpockets at the dog track,
rolling their own cool,
fortune tellers dealing you a morning goddess.

Outside a dance hall, a shadow
retrieves some fag ends to see him through the night;
the musicians snap the lids on their unbuttoned trumpets.

Demon Straightening

While the sea settles for a night on the pebbles,
adulterers in seafront B & Bs put shillings
in the meters to warm the sheets
and whores paint seams on their legs,
down to the heel of their python shoes,
to cast off by the shores of the Metropole.

## Picking Conkers in the Cemetery

Diffused sunlight on leaves, the fine gold dust,
long dark shadows stretch on consecrated
grass where gangs of boys lob sticks to harvest
such a yield; slow work for street wise kids.

I pick up conkers offering them as gifts
to tribal children, to swell their hoards,
like two boys with earrings and shaved heads
struggling with a bag too much for one to lift.

I remember how I used to gather
conkers for my children. We sliced the green
thick, spiky skin, pulled back the pith to wonder
at a doubler, its french polished gleam.

These were picked for combat; the rest stored under beds
where they dulled to rot and grew grey fur.

## *Commodities*
*(With thanks to "The Rise of the Nouveaux Riches" by J. Mordaunt Crook)*


The nouveaux riches are always with us
in various disguises, baroquing their wealth
in fashionable bespoke buildings or just
camping it up with scurrying maids, death
marked by a marble-angelled grave
to remember the climb of diamond miners
and soap supremos, textile and opium
moguls in the Colonies, railways kings, knaves,
waltzed by aristocratic tarts on liners
hard at it to get a good price for a dukedom.
They can't see the colonial son of toil
 shrug his silk suited shoulders and click
on a screen, shifting copper, diamonds, oil
from whence he came, making a killing.

## *Asylum ---shelter, refuge, sanctuary*

He reads the Koran over and over
the story of Yusuf sold into slavery
by his louche brothers.

One old duffle bag of things is
all you can hide in the hold of a ship.
The sailors who found him were kind, he says.

Yusuf's chastity got him thrown into prison.
Prayer and dreams saved him.
He's confused by English girls.

He would like a friend.
He would like to go dancing.
He would like a winter coat.

This is a shabby place, the wind
off a polluted sea. He queues to cash his giro
and dreams of Germany where people drive new cars.

When he prays
he kneels close to the radiator.
The son of the house has called him a fucking Arab.

He misses his youngest brother
and smiles at the kids in the street
but they don't know what to make of him

This is Abdul I say
the slave of God.

## *Edgy*

If you were a vervet monkey you'd curse
in thirty sounds, use more to gossip
till you chutter 'snake' or you could buzz
with triumph as a cicada when you grasp
a female or cagey as a crab extend a claw
to show you're angry but nothing beats
the bee who dances out the route to nectar
but can't show 'up' for flowers in the trees.
Taught or born? a bird that's kept in solitude
can play notes but never sequence them in song;
A child abandoned in a forest can utter sounds
but has no language; a child whose mother tongue
is wrung out, tawdry, harsh, has no words
for walk, no saunter, stroll or stride
just the edgy walk of impenitent kids

## *Demon de Midi*
*(his speciality is to tempt under the guise of doing good)*

Clear of the city
she changed into a mourner
driving with force up an unbelieving lane.

She led the procession
like a bishop, her face torn
with rage, thinking she had invented virtue.

Her children
put hands in their young
pink pockets, while they wondered what was to do.

The midday sun held
a grain of wheat in its palm; not the gate
not the deer, not a mother armed like a butcher, cast a shadow.

The lake sparkled
on the skin of her car. A robin
drank from a puddle, his breast mirrored

back from the water
like a red flower. She silenced
each heart with a knife.

Afterwards
she watched the colour of her children
journey to the evening.

Demon Straightening

She had saved them
from sin and wantoness
but now must save herself.

## Brian Keenan's Orange

*'I am intoxicated by colour. I feel the colour in a quiet
somnambulant rage. Such wonder, such absolute wonder
in an insignificant fruit.'*
-An Evil Cradling, Brian Keenan

In a winter without pigment I try
For colour inside myself but am found
Wanting. The grey of town and sea and sky
Faint in an aquatint of stifled sound.

Some are imprisoned by fear, some by hate;
Others suffocate inside in darkness,
Exiles trapped in yearning for a state
Of intimacy, to close the distance.

But there's a sunset burning in the room;
Its waxy, cool and speckled skin drips oil
When pressed. It sweats a fragrant perfume
Through the strips of pith and gaudy jewel.

I'll let it riot in the dark, consoled
Like Keenan by frankincense and gold.

## Writing in Prison

The Sun King and the Hanged Man
spin their riddles
within walls within walls.
Crossing the yard,
the first breath of air of
a day in a labyrinth.

I am a choirboy singing
the song of the keys
the incantation of sliding locks
the hysterics of seagulls
blown in by a storm.

Today I will be cautious.
Today I will remember
why I am named
and write of the dreams of largactyl.

## Stalked

Delirious shadows are imagined
By candles on the walls of
This gracefully rotting house.
The decomposing shutters
Grunt at night.

Unseen and unheard, wood and plaster
Are gnawed into a new frost on the floor.
A carved sideboard snuffles into debris.
The forest stretches into the bathroom
Embracing pipes, mossing the boards.

The water we haul up is occult.
Forgotten horse hair shifts slowly in its sacks.
Though no-one smokes
We smell Gauloise on our clothes
And the drawers are tripped with trinkets,
A locket from Limoges,
A bone fan, a green rose.

Our pale eyes frighten the earth.
At night our skin sweats like old fly paper
And our shit steams in the forest -
Food for the scrabbling snouts
Shadowed by poised wings.

Demon Straightening

We are other.
We eat nothing that feeds or flies
Through these dank walls
Or hunkers in the corners where we daren't look.

Do the buzzards pick up the
Guttural sound of our snoring
As they float over the crumbling roof?

## FengShui

Space is empty.
Design is loneliness.
The pure arrangement
of the beautiful objects
you have the right to own.

A clutter of knick knacks
buys you remission from purgatory.
Un matching flower-patterned carpets
and wall paper are a full plenary.

A child makes a den
with your feng shui cushions
and mud coloured throws.

The larger the volume of air I claim
the sharper my heart
angled like a Corbusier chair.

## John Clarkson

I was a fatherless boy from solid Cambridgeshire
Righteousness stitched into my linen
Dreaming of battles at sea, honour -
Made a captain's apprentice at thirteen.

When I kept watch in the crow's nest I pulled
Down a piece of sky, learned to read stars,
Splice ropes, furl a sail, polished
The captain's cutlass, learned life from the sailors.

We engaged the French and I saw why everything
Inside was painted scarlet; youthful conceits
Went up in smoke. I loathed the floggings
But loved my ship, a miracle of oak trees.

We waltzed with the Spithead nymphs on shore
Drinking our prize money, toasting the war.

I lost my stomach for the fight, found God
And Abolition. Even sugar tasted now of blood.
My brother tried to preach away the stain
But me, I sailed into their hearts of stone.

I captained the ships, taking freed slaves back
To Africa. A Moses I was called.
I prayed with them when they were sick
With fever. I buried them and distributed land.

There would be harmony, justice, prayer
In the province. I had a white sailor whipped
By a settler. The governors came to stare,
Such drunken failures, rapacious and inept.
Neither fever nor poisoning, which I'd feared
Took me. I returned to marry and die in England.


*Footnote:*
*John Clarkson was a sea-captain, brother of*
*Thomas Clarkson, instigator of the campaign to*
*abolish slavery in the late 18th century.*
*He captained a fleet of ships taking*
*freed slaves to Sierra Leone.*

## Death in the Province of Freedom


We have crawled
Out of the sea, fallen from the sky
Onto the ochre earth, heavy with the dead.

Once we wore hope
Like a cloak, like wings.
Now we crush it into our soup.

A backdrop of infinity
On the stage of the ocean
The tropical rain feels my face with blind fingers.

I lick the ground.
Water, I say, this is water
And my heart palpitates like a mouse heart.

Our seeds are washed
Away into the red rivers.
Even our skin rots like thatch.

Now there is nothing but grief
Ripening on the sludge of the tongue.
Death pursues us faster than a ship in full sail.

We are silent as ash.
Fever cuts off our head as you would snip a rose.
Nothing is more ordinary.
(see footnote on following page)

*Footnote to Death in the Province of Freedom:*

In 1787 four hundred people, mainly former slaves and their wives and children sailed from England to Sierra Leone to found a Utopian community called The Province of Freedom. A third died of fevers within months of arriving.

## The Life of a Sailor

Clearing the Channel a fair wind blew straight
to Madeira where we loaded bullocks and fowl.
Thence to Cape Verde for water and fruit,
Two monkeys and a parakeet; the sea
Still as a duckpond; stars cut in a crystal sky.
We smelt Africa before sighting the coast,
The scent of limes and frangipani.
We were scorched into silence when the sun rose.

Suddenly the weather changed. Rabid
flashes of lightning, the coconut trees
Bent like bows in the rancorous wind.
Typhoons teach man his insignificance.

The ship was wrecked like a beauty after the pox.
We fixed it - throwing overboard our blacks.

Pauline Plummer

## *Straw into Gold*

In Warsaw Danka cut her
length of barley hair
for me to sell for dollars
in a Berlin fair.

Myska's head was pared
by stress. Ashamed
she flew South, grew hair
and changed her name.

In Russia now they
sheave the tresses
of the poor, pack in crates,
for shipping to the West.

A woman haggles roubles
for her mother's chignon
a matt of auburn twists
will buy a chicken.

Unsold and gleaming
under attic beams
lies my honey plait
excised at thirteen

On Saturdays before
the fire my mother washed
and wove this hair round rags;
ringlets for morning mass.

When I was seventeen
I read some Baudelaire
blew smoke into my hair
and learnt to swear.

I wanted a lover
to scour hair across his skin,
thick and coarse
the filaments of brass and tin.

But a man can grab long
hair and drag you back,
can twist your head
until the neck cracks.

After death the hair
stubbornly grows
a flock of goats
buried in the snow.

Long after she had died
a bracelet of white whispy hair
twisted round my mother's
brush till I released it into air.

Pauline Plummer

## Sweet Bleeding Heart

At four I pined for Billy Smith
shipwrecked next door in his bed,
the soft centre of my heart
pinned to my vest, bloody red.

At eight I drummed it
hidden in high wild grass
watching two men through the blades
praying they'd walk past.

As an awkward girl at palais
de danse, petticoat starched to the hips,
quiffed young men sucked my heart
up between my lips.

Just slight affection made me
give of my heart on demand
or throw it on the casino wheel
with a flick of a careless hand.

Until I was nailed to the mast
by a jaunty captain of lies.
We lurched through the storms
in his wake, until we capsized.

You'd think by now the heart
would be through with this stuff
And in sleepless nights you
Call to the moon, enough is enough.

But only your children
can bottle your heart in brine
in a bulging glass held tight
by a clip, a floating valentine.

## Learning to Talk

I didn't speak till I was forty
when words were beaten
into me - eager to please,
dumb, I'd always seemed.

What came out was a call
for help - I learnt to talk
of this and other things
in cadences and form.

Who were my parents?
I've never really known
they didn't tell us stories
of where they'd grown.

In what languages
did our people used to talk
what farms did they leave
why and what did they take?

I took up with someone
adrift whose history
had also been stolen;
two halves jarred to make a person

and lived to tell the tale -just;`
I tell you this because I must.

## Getting my Tongue Round Escaveche

In the photo I'm laughing and transparent
blazing centre stage in a red dress;
your dark hands a pattern on the bodice.
your eyes closed; your head's bent.

It's impossible to see
what you're thinking - the dark room's
dissolved you. Must've been a sweet tune
some lovers' rock to end the party.

Later we'll fall asleep folded
round each other like a marble twist
of brown and cream. Your soul
will fly back to your village and taste

the sweat of water tumbling from
the forest; you'll run along the shore;
and talk with neighbours whom
you haven't seen for twenty years.

In the morning you'll knead dough
for dumplings and simmer them until
the skins are brown and crisp, while
the insides rest soft as snow.

I'll learn to get my tongue round okra
Callalloo and escaveche;
Learn to turn my head away
When voices call from cars, bitch!

I'll get fond of your sisters who'll
 cook me ackee and rice'n'peas.
You'll stay wary of all
my brothers - you'll never trust

a white man and - you'll rip
them off for all you can -this bitter
buried teenage you who always slipped
a knife inside his wind-cheater.

You'll teach me to dance from the hips.
I'll show you the off button on the tv.
We'll spend nights, lip to lip;
Have children wake us sweet and early.

I'll think we're nearly happy, but see how
this other you, like a shadow
on the lungs, will spread and choke
our fragile luck.

## Too many Cowboy Films

When I grew up
I wanted to undress
Behind a screen
Throwing over my flagrant
Petticoats like surf on a roller
While carrying on
A tough conversation
With a cool dude in waistcoat
And chaps
Who stared out the window (honourably)
While catching the flash of white in the reflection
Until he was summoned
With a twist of my red-mouthed head
To hook up my
Scarlet silk shoulder-less dress.

## Uncles and Aunties

I was afraid of uncles,
with laughs like football crowds,
wearing bark coloured clothes,
taking up more space than allowed.

They smelt of cities and work.
Shirts could not contain
the bristles sprouting through collars
and cuffs, the fingers nicotine stained.

A man exposed himself
to me when I was just a kid.
Impossible to tell anyone of his revolting
pinkness, what his flapping trousers hid.

No wonder I preferred aunties -
in their flowery dresses, scrub rough hands,
faces dusted with icing sugar,
permanently permed, lips strawberry jammed.

## Some small Thoughts about Swimming

When I was nine I swam the Thames from side
to side - a bold white form in muddy water.
Taught to swim in local baths by Dad
I preferred a siren's role, to ride
the kicking waves beyond the breakwater
in cold North seas where the seals gather
or dive within the swell of Southern tides
falling through the indigo and jade.

On land the pavements scald my feet, my weight
Sways slow and solid. I dream of gliding
Sleekly; to shed the drudgery in deep
Olive oceans, to feel the ebb against
The rhythm of my heart, my salt skin sliding
Into lapis lazuli like sleep.

Pauline Plummer

## Archeology in Ireland

I came to dig for the secrets
Of my mother's long silences.
I asked the grass for patience
As I entered the valley's
Brooding loop of water
And remembered my mother's
Fierce temper and dark humour.

In this lime-washed farmhouse
Visited a girl with shadows
In the hazel eyes and dark hair;
The strong straight back
In the pony trap to Mass
With freckled peasant hands
Shaped into an arc of prayer.

In country dance halls
My father courted her,
Foxtrotting her to the fiddle.
He loved the craic
But in later life when drunk
Sneered at her plain ways
The Liverpool Irish she spoke.
The back strayed straight.
The confidence broke.

Her people, my people worked
This stony soil on steep fields

Where the farm yards genuflect
In shadow once the sun has fled.
They crossed the water
Settling in choked cities,
at the tail end of the empire
That had made them emigrants
Grafting for booty
To free their children from want.

She thrust us into schooling
The food from which she'd fasted.
Owning nothing
She left as her inheritance
One diamond ring
And random bits of Irishness
Wrapped in the gift of Faith
To wear as warm coat
Vivid dress and straightjacket.

In old age she despaired
At all the prayers fallen
On stony ground unheard;
Grief ran like a fault line
Through her to me and back
To a place we once belonged
Loved but also hostile
Where I try to catch an old song
In the wind like one beguiled.

## Looking for Myth
*(For Brigid and Robert)*

A green silk Atlantic laps the stones
Panning for quartz; behind a deformed island
In the scorched haze, a seal's lamentation
I've come looking for myth in Malin Head.

A country bar, propped up by men in work-worn
Tweed, white hair nicotined - my English grammar
Noticed, nudged - a strange one this woman alone
Spread on beaches, reading Kavanagh

The hills of Donegal are on fire, red
Waves and black smoke against a sunset's fever.
I hitch a ride with Robert and Brigid
Who love across Faith's bitter frontier.

They ask and watch the answers on my face
Mirrored in the checkpoint glass.

## A Cool Hand

he'll
crack an egg lightly on the side of the cooker
just enough to let yolk and white slide through
the jagged edges into the soft pile of flour
slightly grey in the evening light
and mix
pouring milk in with one hand
holding a long spliff in his other
keeping the ash away from the open face of the bowl
while speaking over his shoulder to Sister Marie
who wants to know why the boy's
been missing so much school.
There's education and there's education, sister,
and then he'll flick a wedge of pale butter
into the hot rusting pan on too high a flame
and jerk in a stream of mix
and catch it burning into brown blisters
to be flicked over with one hand
resettling the spliff in his mouth
with the other.

Pauline Plummer

## *Babe*

Heroic in her cascade of Geordie perm,
her exquisitely embroidered bra-top
embellished in her cycling shorts.

Club lights sparkle
on her stunning carat gold skin tones.
The salt at the edge of her tequila
tastes of sweat.

Imagine her excitement
entrancing the handsome stranger,
the devil in designer soft top.

He spins his trainers
in authentic spectaculars
and in delightful anticipation
relishes the superb detail of the tattoo on her shoulder.

Speaking in block capitals
in a meticulously researched settee
he leaves his signature on her flowered fan
on a no-obligation basis.

## A Stanza for Peter
## On the Occasion of his Forty Ninth Birthday

We tried on a paradigm of isms.
Some of which rubbed like hair-shirts
and others brought a kind of wisdom
that came from failure and hurt.
The fifties world we came from felt
stifling - its fearful decencies, Bible and belt.
We crossed borders and craved
spontaneity in our brave new world.
We'd bury our parents' sad marriages
with love lent out and taken back
when sour . Owning only luck
and doubt we thought we'd manage.
Jericho did not come crumbling down
but you still tap your drum.

(For Peter Lammimam)

## *In the Salon*

While I buffed his immaculate nails
I sized up the rows of transplanted hair,
The designer immaculate clothes
Paid for by months on the rigs.

When his wife and the kids were away
I glued on the lash extensions
Nothing too brash - and slipped him
A bit of remover, in case.

In the intimacy of the booth
With the cloying smell of melting wax
As I wrenched off his leg hair in strips
He told me about the lingerie bought for his wife.

How he snapped into her basque
And slipped on something cool
And cobwebbed while she clacked away
Into her own face in the monitor.

He likes our new line in varnish
The warm blush colours
And the artificial tan mousse.
Go on try it, I said, but he's not sure.

## Breathless

She met him at a tea dance;
in her fifties make-up,
roots like early snowdrops,
passing for sixty.

Retired from something in chemicals,
He drove a Blue-Bird too fast,
Wore a dapper moustache,
Cravate in the neck of his recently-widowed shirts.
A friend big in investments had let him down.

En route for Florida, the captain married them.
Her son shredded the telegramme.

She censored the blood pressure and
in corsets and new dresses, quick-stepped
till her ankles swelled,
gin taking the pain away somewhere.

Jerked in and out of taxis,
the heat melting her Coty mask,
someone even more stubborn
than she, ran with her handbag.

'Stroke' dotted out the fax.
'Her face petrified' he told them at the club.
Well, it was blue.

## Sailing on Single Beds
*(For Tom and Kathleen)*

Unsteady and curved, washed, turned and fed,
Looted their strength not robbed of their humour,
They take exception to their single beds,
With handrails and hoists and pads for tumours.

Like pitch and pine and brick and mortar, they
Support each other in the final test
Of their humanity; How to bear the day
When one's left stateless waiting for the next?

A veined hand pats a frozen hand. A touch rewards
For sixty years of double bed, skin smells,
Hair, the rhythm of familiar words.
Separately they hoist their sheets, crisp sails,
Float like Lazarus, strong and whole again
To soar beyond the season's requiem.

## Mother and Daughters

First she tested her elbow in the water
in a sink; thin towel warming
to dry the first born daughter.

This was her first dark thread of kin.
Another daughter was born, blonde
and blue-eyed - the mother was overfond.

The first daughter married a local lad;
the other a man with a career,
a company car and manicured hands.

He moved her accent into a nice area
where mother couldn't drop in
though of course it was lovely to see her.

Mother became a grandma, with skin
like the crust on a pie - she preferred
bairns doing well who hardly saw her.

*Why am I left with the daughter
in the shabby house, the quiet one
who shampoos and brushes my hair?*

She grips the stick with knuckle bones
shaping words out of air to cast as stones.

## Mike At Fifty

In a lotus eating summer of privilege
someplace between sleep and awake
a clever boy and a girl a bit damaged
looked up from a guitar and spoke.

You rode down life with a six shooter full
of certainties - couldn't see you for smoke,
out front, sheriff and outlaw in one hell
of a showdown between the cant and the comic.

Who knows what pulls friendship through
travels, marriages, jobs?  I drifted engrossed
in doubts and caprice but  somehow the glue
of shared liking, culture, the past kept us close.

Perhaps, we've both tried to make a difference
but without a loss of faith in kindness.

## Lonely Hearts

You've swigged a miniature of vodka
to meet him over tea
biting into cake with your first communion teeth.

You toss him a few questions
but the lost lover slung
on his shoulder crushes his windpipe

Your head's been pared to the skull
and he's as brittle as a mummy
with sealed eyes.

He walks you to the castle
points out a medieval woodcarving,
a man pushing a woman in a wheelbarrow. You both laugh.

Down steps, in the chill of the stone chapel,
a thousand years of prayer are sap in the pillars
and you want him to touch, the sign of his thumb.

You're the same decade, so you spill song lyrics
on your beer mats and gossip about someone you both know
but know nothing about.

Though you could plot laughter and picnics
you guess he wants magic for the resurrection.
The words you could have said rush to catch their train.

## Slicing Aubergines

We have never stood as close.
Better to concentrate on slicing aubergines
plump as bull's balls.

It's safer to pare the crocodile skin off a cucumber
dicing the pale green flesh
than think of the suck of your blasphemous tongue;
peel the crisp skins off an onion
like pulling a freshly ironed shirt
over your shoulders.

The melon pulp sweats stains in the crook of your thumb
but I must not attempt to lick it clean
or dip my fingers in the flux of coconut milk
and rub them along the edges of your teeth.

## Swimming in the Irish Sea

Longing and shame dip and soar with the swallows
I have exiled desire on the rocks
For you are so young, a mhian.

But it washes in with the swilling tide.
Under a full moon my palms cleave its milk;
longing and shame dip and soar with the swallows.

I scissor and kick legs against the ebb
my skin stinging with such salt cold penance
For you are so young, a mhian.

In the long way back to shore you flail the waves
I could wrap you in legs and drag you down,
longing and shame dip and soar with the swallows.

You circle me with a shark fin of a shoulder;
I could swallow you, bark your taste from inside my fur
For you are so young, a mhian.

Though my eyes are secret as the morning sea
I should walk on my knees across a mile of pebbles
Shame and longing dip and soar
for you are so young, a mhian.

Irish word: a mhian - my desire

## Walking Out

Say, in twenty years, you'll reminisce
to a friend how when you were young
you loved a woman in a red dress
old enough to be your mother, a headstrong
foreigner who mapped in languid
lines your body for you - how you travelled
after abstinence, how she was liquid
tilting like a ship's lamp in the swell.

You refused to walk out with her, hid
your secret but in moonlight knelt against
her, mouth devouring shadowed breast
stroked by veigned and jewelled hands .

By then you'll wear a salad sprig of mistress
in your button hole to raise your status.

## R & R

How you watched me through your night sight-spilling
The beans, This is my life, dared me to care -
My gander in black and tan abseiling
In from Aran, sparrow hawks in your hair.

Your bite was soft as gas. You liked worn
Out glamour, seductive and maternal
To press your bony frame against again
Again. To hell with any scandal.

You were all  speed and half rations fasting
To be hard, to survive Belfast, the Gulf,
The swamps of Belize - danger wasting
Your capacity to love - sex was enough.

Once you'd searched for your mother, and left,
Then found your father but watched and wept.

## Dunfermline

You watch behind the hibernian nets
for the muttering of my stirling engine,
my heart of midlothian.

Declaring a truce on the partick thistles
in your garden, you become
a hamiltonian on a deckchair,
with ale and dundees.

You were a lone academical,
airdrie over the hedges for a winger.

    But now
    I am your celtic,
    spotted in green silk the other side of a party,
You, rangers, and cautious.

## Café Tinto

Years of stowing away in foreign wars,
women scattered along the way like stones
to find his way home, his Bogota manners
intact, he turned up, still cool, a little worn.

*Remember we used to be lovers* he said
*Come back with me to my mountains,
fight the good fight in forgotten crusades* .
I poured coffee in my green garden, uncertain.

The rose and fruit trees cast long mauve
shadows like the years between our young selves
who dreamed of sharing rice with the Buddha
and the people we'd become, scarred and harder.

We made love to say farewell, like the courteous
strangers we were, attentive, in our forties.

## *Porque Tenemos Deseo? Because we are alone*
*(Graffiti seen in London)*

Hiding from the boys in the garage
you roll desire in the neatest spliff
I've ever seen.
*Will they never go to sleep?*
The valve on the pressure cooker forces out small tears.

Weeks later you phone
as I skin a chicken for tea.
You say
in a garlic and lime accent
*I'm going to eat you when I see you.*

I follow you upstairs
floating islands in my head.
You sit and push against me, silent,
rolling each breast along the sides of your face.
My mouth has bitten into raw chili.

## Buying a Blouse That Fits

Newspapers are flying
about the icy streets.
We drink warm beer
while ghosts in the juke box
serenade our broken faith.

The Thai waitress gives you
one of those are you pleased with my smile smiles
and after coffee
the manager asks you
*do you want boys or girls?
Ah, the English are so cold, no?*

*You're going grey.
Have I aged?*, I ask.
I lie about my size
but you buy me a blouse that fits anyway.

In the train the couple opposite
tear into each other
like a trapped bear biting off its paw.
Later in the hotel
you try my skin against yours for size.

## You are the one my Womb Loves Best
*(line from Sumerian religious song)*

Your shoulder is a scythe
Reaping in moonlight
Your ribs are a curragh
Before the waves
I can press the hollow of your stomach with one hand
Your legs are shares on the plough's axis
Riddles are inscribed on the parchment of your back
Inside your mouth I taste molluscs and butterflies
Your eyes are alder bark
Sprinkled with myrtle
Spun in your arms
I breathe high altitudes and euphoria
Pluck out my eye I can only see you as a man
Your skin is the cloth I am wrapped in
I drink the honey milk
Of my familiar and I do not possess myself
On the tabor of your sex
We play intemperate music
You are the one my womb loves best

## What Like is Love ?

Is there a route through the labyrinth?
Running through passages,
Pulse improvising a tortuous solo,
A blackbird beating against the glass.

Is there a minotaur at the core?
A ribcage for rutting,
Moonlight on the dark, coarse hair -
or a poor forked animal,
Whistling against the dark,
Signing the limestone with his handprint?

What dowry shall I bring?
Trinkets from other decades,
The Queen of smiles,
A small boy wrapped inside my coat,
An amulet of metaphors.

What is your bride price?
Rapture and skin heat,
learning and laughter,
Drumbeats on the spine,
Chrysanthemums at sunrise?

To whom do you pray
And who is your God,
Eros or Agape?

Pauline Plummer

## *Swansong for the Womb*

We are a row of women
without wombs;
silent, letting go.

The surgeons have stripped our
cavities and pouches,
have scraped and gutted their trout,
bled us clean, Kosher, Halal,
skimmed off our sins,
stitched up erotic dreams
inside our black wool.

We are gourds,
mangos without stones,
a row of matrioskas.

All our seeds have been sown -
nothing stored against siege and famine;
if there are tares in the wheat
then we will eat each other
or hallucinate with hunger.

Once we were pomegranates,
with the callous patina of youth
popping with bitter seeds in sweet juice.
Now we are plump as late sloes,
our spittle tasting of wrack,
novices in a late vocation.

## Strictly Tempo

He's light footed, my Dad.
Forbidden football glamour
by a fiercely Welsh father
he quickstepped his way into trade.

In the dance halls of Liverpool
he foxtrotted mother off her feet,
converted to marry her and closed
behind him the door of Chapel.

Called up to war, he lent his grace
to blowing up bridges; slow waltzed
across the Rhine on a raft of corpses,
A fact he wrapped in silence.

His Croix de Guerre hung framed -
unbelievable - our ordinary Dad
had fought in battles.
I've heard him tell the lost names.

The demobbed stranger returned
to resentful sons and the awkward
tango of married life.  The old tempo
of trade was the one in which he burned

to win, learning the moves and slides
to the percussion of whisky and ice,
the softened accent in the golf club,
the cliches of blazers and phony ties.

Pauline Plummer

I remember odd intimate scenes -
he held her foot and pared her corns
with a razor ; the flight of his descant
at mass;  him teaching me to dance.

The wit and quick tongue dressed
a temper.  On the move from town to town
they fought to fierce crescendos.  I banged
my head against a wall to make it pass.

Widowers at  dances prefer
a flashy partner.  I've watched him
trying to lurch to rock - a loss of style
no glide of soft shoe into air.

He doesn't like old photographs
now he's given up on Mass,
can't remember how to speak in Welsh
or what it was that drove him to such wrath.

## News from Burkina Faso

Last thing at night
I check the pick-axe
hidden behind the laundry basket.

In case it explodes
I unplug the TV
as my brother has told me to do.

I take the key out of the front door
so the young men of the house
can return without smashing the door down,

hoping  they return sober enough
to make it to bed, without having
picked up any stray dogs on the way.

It's a toss up whether the  mutt
will be allowed to sleep on the bed.
Clean duvet or the  murmur of  dog breath?

The World Service bringing  news from Burkina Faso
 or the Nina SimoneCD?
Midnight 's decisions.

You listen to next door's chair lift,
a cat on the prowl,
the pulse of your own heart